Siddha Stotra Mālā

With kind regards, ॐ and prem

Swami Niranjan

Siddha Stotra Mālā

Garland of Chants

Yoga Publications Trust, Munger, Bihar, India

Published by Yoga Publications Trust
1st edition 2004
Reprinted 2005

ISBN: 81-86336-37-0

Publisher and distributor: Yoga Publications Trust, Ganga Darshan, Munger, Bihar, India.

Printed at Thomson Press (India) Limited, New Delhi, 110001

SWAMI SIVANANDA SARASWATI

Swami Sivananda was born at Pattamadai, Tamil Nadu, in 1887. After serving as a medical doctor in Malaya, he renounced his practice, went to Rishikesh and was initiated into Dashnami sannyasa in 1924 by Swami Vishwananda Saraswati. He toured extensively throughout India, inspiring people to practise yoga and lead a divine life. He founded the Divine Life Society at Rishikesh in 1936, the Sivananda Ayurvedic Pharmacy in 1945, the Yoga Vedanta Forest Academy in 1948 and the Sivananda Eye Hospital in 1957. During his lifetime Swami Sivananda guided thousands of disciples and aspirants all over the world and authored over 200 books.

SWAMI SATYANANDA SARASWATI

Swami Satyananda was born at Almora, Uttar Pradesh, in 1923. In 1943 he met Swami Sivananda in Rishikesh and adopted the Dashnami sannyasa way of life. In 1955 he left his guru's ashram to live as a wandering mendicant and later founded the International Yoga Fellowship in 1956 and the Bihar School of Yoga in 1963. Over the next 20 years Swami Satyananda toured internationally and authored over 80 books. In 1987 he founded Sivananda Math, a charitable institution for aiding rural development, and the Yoga Research Foundation. In 1988 he renounced his mission, adopting kshetra sannyasa, and now lives as a paramahamsa sannyasin.

SWAMI NIRANJANANANDA SARASWATI

Swami Niranjanananda was born in Madhya Pradesh in 1960. At the age of four he joined the Bihar School of Yoga and was initiated into Dashnami sannyasa at the age of ten. From 1971 he travelled overseas and toured many countries for the next 11 years. In 1983 he was recalled to India and appointed President of Bihar School of Yoga. Since then he has guided the development of Ganga Darshan, Sivananda Math, Yoga Publications Trust and the Yoga Research Foundation. In 1990 he was initiated as a paramahamsa and in 1993 anointed preceptor in succession to Swami Satyananda. Bihar Yoga Bharati was founded under his direction in 1994. He has authored over 20 books and guides national and international yoga programs.

SWAMI SATYASANGANANDA SARASWATI

Swami Satyasangananda (Satsangi) was born on 24th March 1953, in Chandorenagore, West Bengal. From the age of 22 she experienced a series of inner awakenings which led her to her guru, Swami Satyananda. From 1981 she travelled ceaselessly with her guru in India and overseas and developed into a scholar with deep insight into the yogic and tantric traditions as well as modern sciences and philosophies. She is an efficient channel for the transmission of her guru's teachings. The establishment of Sivananda Math in Rikhia is her creation and mission, and she guides all its activities there, working tirelessly to uplift the weaker and underprivileged areas. She embodies compassion with clear reason and is the foundation of her guru's vision.

Contents

Phonetic Pronunciation Guide

अ		a	*as in* up
आ	ा	ā	far
इ	ि	i	hill
ई	ी	ī	free
उ	ु	u	pull
ऊ	ू	ū	fool
ऋ		ṛ	rip
ॠ	ृ	ṝ	marine
ऌ		lṛ	rivalry
ॡ		lṝ	rivalry (*prolonged*)
ए	े	e	grey
ऐ	ै	ai	ape
ओ	ो	o	on
औ	ौ	au	or
ं		ṃ	rum
ः		ḥ	ah
क्		k	king
ख्		kh	inkhorn
ग्		g	go
घ्		gh	yoghurt
ङ्		ṅ	sing
च्		ch	check
छ्		chh	churchhill
ज्		j	joy
झ्		jh	hedgehog
ञ्		ñ	canyon

ट्	ṭ	true
ठ्	ṭh	anthill
ड्	ḍ	do
ढ्	ḍh	redhead
ण्	ṇ	gone
त्	t	water (*dental*)
थ्	th	nuthook
द्	d	do
ध्	dh	adhere (*more dental*)
न्	n	not
प्	p	pay
फ्	ph	photo
ब्	b	rub
भ्	bh	abhor
म्	m	map
य्	y	yoga
र्	r	red
ल्	l	love
व्	v	victory
श्	ś	shiva
ष	ṣ	assure
स्	s	sun
ह्	h	hit
क्ष्	kṣ	rickshaw
त्र्	tr	track (*dental*)
ज्ञ्	jñ	gyana

Introduction

How do we reach the Atman, or innermost self, which is beyond the senses, the mind or any other means at our disposal? Do we have any idea what this Self is like? The Upanishads declare, *"Naiva vacha na manasa praptum"*: The Self cannot be reached by speech or mind. Fortunately the saints and sages who have established themselves in the state of fullness and realization have given us some indications. They described the state of *ananda,* or bliss, which leads to an outpouring of that experience in the form of a stotra or hymn. The word *stotra* literally means a collection of mantras which glorifies the supreme reality, as in *Purusha Suktam,* a vedic hymn which describes one specific power of the supreme reality, or *Vishnu Sahasranam,* where the focus is on omnipresence. In this way, regular chanting of the stotras allows one to remember the divine and actually get the feeling of that experience.

A stotra is an expression of that higher state of consciousness, where connection is established with the heart, the centre of feeling. In the Sanatana tradition, a very important place is accorded to stotras as a means of awakening *bhavana*, the faculty of pure feeling. By establishing a strong connection with the heart, we are able to experience shakti, the cosmic dimension of creation, the divine power that manifests, sustains and transforms the universe, as the one unifying force of existence. In this light, Swami Sivananda says, "Devi stotras are powerful reservoirs of mantra. Every verse is a dynamic force which acts powerfully to overhaul the nature of man."

All stotras are revelations of the sages and rishis. The main sources of the stotras are the Vedas, Puranas, Tantras and other smriti texts, which were transmitted by memory. The tradition of *upasana*, or ceremonial worship, also utilizes stotras as a tool.

Adiguru Shankaracharya composed a great number of stotras. There are interesting episodes related to many of these stotras. For example, Hastamalaka, one of Shankara's four main disciples, never spoke or showed any interest in normal activities. His father brought the boy to Shankara, who asked him, "Who are you?" Out came the most sublime poetry and expression of the state he was in: "I am not man, god, householder, forest dweller, brahmin or kshatriya, but I am pure awareness alone . . . I am that eternal, undifferentiated consciousness." This utterance later became an important stotra of the vedantic tradition.

Stotras are a means to transmit spiritual teachings through the vibrations of mantra. For example, *Bhaja Govindam* by Shankaracharya is a stotra which awakens *vairagya*, or non-attachment. Stotras are also a reflection of the eternal truth that the 'name' is greater than God. There are so many names for the different powers of the creator, for example, Shiva, Vishnu, Lalita, Rama, Krishna etc. *Naam Ramayana* is an example of the glory of the name of Rama. Similarly such stotras as *Shiva Mahimna, Vishnu Sahasranam* or *Lalita Sahasranam* fulfil this purpose.

Mantra shastra tells us that there is mystical energy encapsulated in the form of sound. It is possible to awaken that energy through the practice of mantras. Swami Sivananda used to prescribe 'namopathy' when the other therapies failed. He said, "There is an inscrutable power or shakti in the Lord's name. All divine potencies are hidden in the Lord's name." This is because mantra takes one through the different levels of sound frequency from the external spoken word, or *vaikhari*, to the transcendental level of *para*, the undifferentiated potential sound which is the unchanging primal substratum of all language and energy. Para is *shabda brahman*, or shakti, pure energy.

This collection of stotras is a very special offering to the many forms of the divine, and has the blessings of the siddhas and saints of all eras. These hymns give the sadhaka a gentle push by softening and opening up the heart and elevating the mind and consciousness, so that the presence of God can be explained as a palpable reality in one's own spiritual life.

Guru Stotra

Guru-pādukā-stotram

1. Anantasaṃsārasamudratāra-
Naukāyitābhyāṃ gurubhaktidābhyām.
Vairāgyasāmrājyadapūjanābhyām
Namo namaḥ śrīgurupādukābhyām.

2. Kavitvavārāśiniśākarābhyām
Daurbhāgyadāvāmbudamālikābhyām.
Dūrīkṛtānamravipattitābhyām
Namo namaḥ śrīgurupādukābhyām.

3. Natā yayoḥ śrīpatitāṃ samīyuḥ
Kadāchidapyāśu daridravaryāḥ.
Mūkāścha vāchaspatitāṃ hi tābhyām
Namo namaḥ śrīgurupādukābhyām.

4. Nālīkanīkāśapadāhṛtābhyām
Nānāvimohādi nivārikābhyām.
Namajjanābhīṣṭatatipradābhyām
Namo namaḥ śrīgurupādukābhyām.

5. Nṛpālimaulivrajaratnakānti-
Saridvirājajjhaṣakanyakābhyām.
Nṛpatvadābhyāṃ natalokapaṅkteḥ
Namo namaḥ śrīgurupādukābhyām.

6. Pāpāndhakārārka paramparābhyām
Tāpatrayāhīndrakhageśvarābhyām.
Jāḍyābdhisaṃśoṣaṇavāḍavābhyām
Namo namaḥ śrīgurupādukābhyām.

7. Śamādiṣaṭkapradavaibhavābhyām
Samādhidānavratadīkṣitābhyām.
Ramādhavāṅghristhirabhaktidābhyām
Namo namaḥ śrīgurupādukābhyām.

8. Svārchāparāṇāmakhileṣṭadābhyām
Svāhāsahāyākṣadhurandharābhyām.
Svāntāchchhabhāvaprada pūjanābhyām
Namo namaḥ śrīgurupādukābhyām.

9. Kāmādisarpavrajagāruḍābhyām
Vivekavairāgyanidhipradābhyām.
Bodhapradābhyāṃ drutamokṣadābhyām
Namo namaḥ śrīgurupādukābhyām.

Guru-stotram

1. Akhaṇḍamaṇḍalākāraṃ vyāptaṃ yena charācharam.
Tatpadaṃ darśitaṃ yena tasmai śrī gurave namaḥ.

2. Ajñānatimirāndhasya jñānāñjanaśalākayā.
Chakṣurunmīlitaṃ yena tasmai śrī gurave namaḥ.

3. Gururbrahmā gururviṣṇuḥ gururdevo maheśvaraḥ.
Guruḥ sākṣāt paraṃbrahma tasmai śrī gurave namaḥ.

4. Sthāvaraṃ jaṅgamaṃ vyāptaṃ yatkiñchit sacharācharam.
Tatpadaṃ darśitaṃ yena tasmai śrī gurave namaḥ.

5. Chinmayaṃ vyāpitaṃ sarvaṃ trailokyaṃ sacharācharaṃ.
Tatpadaṃ darśitaṃ yena tasmai śrī gurave namaḥ.

6. Sarvaśrutiśiroratna virājitapadāmbujaḥ.
Vedāntāmbujasūryāya tasmai śrī gurave namaḥ.

7. Chaitanyaṃ śāśvataṃ śāntaṃ vyomātītaṃ nirañjanaḥ.
Bindunādakalātītaḥ tasmai śrī gurave namaḥ.

8. Jñānaśakti-samārūḍhaḥ tattva-mālā vibhūṣitaḥ.
Bhukti-mukti-pradātā cha tasmai śrī gurave namaḥ.

9. Aneka janmasamprāpta karmabandhavidāhine.
Ātmajñāna pradānena tasmai śrī gurave namaḥ.

10. Śoṣaṇaṃ bhava-sindhoścha jñāpanaṃ sāra-sampadaḥ.
Gurorpādodakaṃ samyak tasmai śrī gurave namaḥ.

11. Na guroradhikaṃ tattvaṃ na guroradhikaṃ tapaḥ.
Tattva-jñānāt paraṃ nāsti tasmai śrī gurave namaḥ.

12. Mannāthaḥ śrī jagannāthaḥ madguruḥ śrī jagadguruḥ.
Madātmā sarvabhūtātmā tasmai śrī gurave namaḥ.

13. Gururādiranādiścha guruḥ parama-daivatam.
Guroḥ parataraṃ nāsti tasmai śrī gurave namaḥ.

14. Dhyānamūlaṃ gurormūrttiḥ pūjāmūlaṃ gurorpadam.
Mantramūlaṃ gurorvākyaṃ mokṣamūlaṃ gurorkṛpā.

Śrī-guru-stutiḥ

1. Netinetītyādi nigamavachanena
Nipuṇaṃ nijidhyamūrtāmūrtarāśim.
Yadaśakyanihnatvaṃ svātmarūpatayā
Jānanti kovidāstattvamasi tattvam.

2. Khādyamutpādyaviśvamanupraviśya
Gūḍhamannamayādikośatuṣajāle.
Kavayovivichya yuktyavaghātato
Yattaṇḍulavadādadati tattvamasi tattvam.

3. Viṣamaviṣayeṣu sañchāriṇo'kṣāśvān
Doṣadarśana kaśābhighātataḥ.
Svairaṃ sannivartya svāntaraśmibhirdhīrā
Badhnanti yatra tattvamasi tattvam.

4. Vyāvṛttajāgradādiṣvanusyūtaṃ
Tebhyo'nyadivapuṣpebhya iva sūtram.
Iti yadaupādhikatrayapṛthakatvena
Vidantisūrayastattvamasi tattvam.

5. Puruṣa evedamityādivedeṣu
Sarvakāraṇatayā yasya sārvātmyam.
Hāṭakasyeva mukuṭādi tādātmyam
Sarasamāmnāyate tattvamasi tattvam.

6. Yaśchāhamatravarṣmaṇi bhāmiso'sau
Yo'sau vibhāti ravimaṇḍale so'hamiti.
Vedavādino vyatihārato yaddhyāpayanti
Yatnatastattvamasi tattvam.

7. Vedānuvachanasaddānamukha dharmaiḥ
Śraddhayā'nuṣṭhitairvidyayā yuktaiḥ.
Vividiṣantyatyantavimalasvāntā
Brāhmaṇā yadbrahma tattvamasi tattvam.

8. Śamadamoparamādi sādhanairdhīrāḥ
Svātmanā''tmani yadanviṣya kṛtakṛtyāḥ.
Adhigatāmita sachchidānandarūpā
Na punarihakhidyante tattvamasi tattvam.

Gurvaṣṭakam

1. Śarīraṃ surūpaṃ tathā vā kalatraṃ
Yaśaśchāru chitraṃ dhanaṃ merutulyam.
Guroḥ pāda padme manaśchenna lagnaṃ
Tataḥ kiṃ tataḥ kiṃ tataḥ kiṃ tataḥ kim.

2. Kalatraṃ dhanaṃ putrapautrādi sarvaṃ
Gṛhaṃ bāndhavāḥ sarvametaddhi jātam.
Guroḥ pāda padme manaśchenna lagnaṃ
Tataḥ kiṃ tataḥ kiṃ tataḥ kiṃ tataḥ kim.

3. Ṣaḍaṅgādivedo mukhe śāstravidyā,
Kavitvādi gadyaṃ supadyaṃ karoti.
Guroḥ pāda padme manaśchenna lagnaṃ
Tataḥ kiṃ tataḥ kiṃ tataḥ kiṃ tataḥ kim.

4. Videśeṣu mānyaḥ svadeśeṣu dhanyaḥ,
Sadāchāravṛtteṣu matto na chānyaḥ.
Guroḥ pāda padme manaśchenna lagnaṃ
Tataḥ kiṃ tataḥ kiṃ tataḥ kiṃ tataḥ kim.

5. Kṣamāmaṇḍale bhūpabhūpālavṛndaiḥ
Sadā sevitaṃ yasya pādāravindam.
Guroḥ pāda padme manaśchenna lagnaṃ
Tataḥ kiṃ tataḥ kiṃ tataḥ kiṃ tataḥ kim.

6. Yaśo me gataṃ dikṣu dānapratāpāt-
Jagadvastu sarvaṃ kare yatprasādāt.
Guroḥ pāda padme manaśchenna lagnaṃ
Tataḥ kiṃ tataḥ kiṃ tataḥ kiṃ tataḥ kim.

7. Na bhoge na yoge na vā vājirājau,
Na kāntāmukhe naiva vitteṣu chittam.
Guroḥ pāda padme manaśchenna lagnaṃ
Tataḥ kiṃ tataḥ kiṃ tataḥ kiṃ tataḥ kim.

8. Araṇye na vā svasya gehe na kārye,
Na dehe mano vartate me tvanarghye.
Guroḥ pāda padme manaśchenna lagnaṃ
Tataḥ kiṃ tataḥ kiṃ tataḥ kiṃ tataḥ kim.

Śivānanda Maṅgalam

1. Sadā pāvanī jāhnavītīravāsiṃ
Sadā svasvarūpānusandhānaśīlam.
Sadā suprasannaṃ dayāluṃ bhaje'haṃ
Śivānandayogīndramānandamūrttim.

2. Harerdivyanāmaṃ svayaṃ kīrtayantaṃ
Hareḥ pādabhaktiṃ sadā bodhayantam.
Hareḥ pādapadmasthabhṛṅgaṃ bhaje'haṃ
Śivānandayogīndramānandamūrttim.

3. Jarāvyādhidaurbalyasampīḍitānāṃ
Sadā''rogyadaṃ yasya kāruṇyanetram.
Bhaje'haṃ samastārttasevādhurīṇaṃ
Śivānandayogīndramānandamūrttim.

4. Sadā nirvikalpe sthiraṃ yasya chittaṃ
Sadākumbhitaḥ prāṇavāyurnikāmam.
Sadāyoganiṣṭhaṃ nirīhaṃ bhaje'haṃ
Śivānandayogīndramānandamūrttim.

5. Mahāmudrābandhādiyogāṅgadakṣaṃ
Suṣumnāntare chitsvarūpe nimagnam.
Mahāyoganidrā-vilīnaṃ bhaje'haṃ
Śivānandayogīndramānandamūrttim.

6. Dayāsāgaraṃ sarvakalyāṇarāśiṃ
Sadā sachchidānandarūpe nilīnam.
Sadāchāraśīlaṃ bhaje'ham bhaje'ham
Śivānandayogīndramānandamūrttim.

7. Bhavāmbhodhinaukānibhaṃ yasya netraṃ
Mahāmohaghorāndhakāraṃ harantam.
Bhaje'haṃ sadā taṃ mahāntaṃ nitāntaṃ
Śivānandayogīndramānandamūrttim.

8. Bhaje'haṃ jagatkāraṇaṃ satsvarūpaṃ
Bhaje'haṃ jagadvyāpakaṃ chitsvarūpam.
Bhaje'haṃ nijānandamānandarūpaṃ
Śivānandayogīndramānandamūrttim.